My Garden ♥ Planner

Journal and Log Book

By

Endless Journals

https://endlessjournals.com

This Planner Belongs To:

Name: _____

Address: _____

Email: _____

Phone: _____

Gardening Year

_____

❧ Contents ☙

PLANNING

Welcome to my Garden

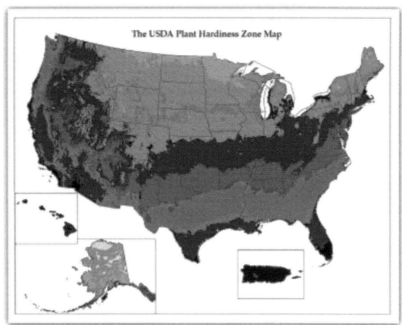

The USDA Plant Hardiness Zone Map

Average Annual Extreme Minimum Temperature 1976-2005		
Temp (F)	Zone	Temp (C)
-60 to -50	1	-51.1 to -45.6
-50 to -40	2	-45.6 to -40
-40 to -30	3	-40 to -34.4
-30 to -20	4	-34.4 to -28.9
-20 to -10	5	-28.9 to -23.3
-10 to 0	6	-23.3 to -17.8
0 to 10	7	-17.8 to -12.2
10 to 20	8	-12.2 to -6.7
20 to 30	9	-6.7 to -1.1
30 to 40	10	-1.1 to 4.4
40 to 50	11	4.4 to 10
50 to 60	12	10 to 15.6
60 to 70		15.6 to 21.1

packets and plant tags. Since the release of the AHS Heat Zone Map in 1997, over 15,000 plants have been coded for heat tolerance, with more on the way.

The USDA Plant Hardiness Zone Map

Are You Using the Latest Version? In 1990 the U.S. Department of Agriculture (USDA) published the USDA Plant Hardiness Zone Map as an aid in determining which plants will thrive in the average *lowest* temperatures of a region. It was based on weather data from only a 13-year time period (1974-1986).

In 2012 the USDA released new updated Plant Hardiness Zone Maps for the United States, each state and geographical region, and Puerto Rico.

If you have been using the older map you may find a shift in your zone. The zones in the new map are, in general, about 5°F warmer, although some mountainous regions are cooler. The change is due to data being taken from more weather stations and for a longer period of time. Two new zones were added: Zone 12 and Zone 13. They apply to Hawaii and Puerto Rico.

For More Info: ** https://planthardiness.ars.usda.gov **

Plant Hardiness
Last & First Frost Dates

Average Frost Dates For United States

City	Last Spring Frost	First Fall Frost	City	Last Spring Frost	First Fall Frost
Albuquerque, NM	Apr 13	Oct 28	Duluth, MN	May 22	Sept 24
Ashville, NC	Apr 12	Oct 24	Eugene, OR	Apr 13	Nov 24
Atlanta, GA	Mar 21	Nov 18	Grand Rapids, MI	Apr 23	Oct 30
Baltimore, MD	Mar 28	Nov 19	GT. Falls, MT	May 9	Sept 25
Bangor, ME	May 1	Oct 4	Harrisburg, PA	Apr 9	Oct 30
Birmingham, AL	Mar 19	Nov 14	Hartford, CT	Apr 22	Oct 19
Bismarck, ND	May 11	Sept 24	Houston, TX	Mar 14	Nov 21
Boise, ID	Apr 23	Oct 17	Indianapolis, IN	Apr 13	Oct 27
Boston, MA	Apr 5	Nov 8	Kansas City, MO	Apr 6	Oct 30
Buffalo, NY	Apr 30	Oct 25	Las Vegas, NV	Mar 16	Nov 10
Burlington, VT	May 8	Oct 3	Lexington, KY	Apr 13	Oct 28
Caribou, ME	May 19	Sept 21	Little rock, AR	Mar 17	Nov 13
Charleston, SC	Feb 19	Dec 10	Los Angelis, CA	Jan 3	Dec 28
Charleston, WV	Apr 18	Oct 28	Lubbock, TX	Apr 1	Nov 9
Cheyenne, WY	May 14	Oct 3	Memphis, TN	Mar 20	Nov 12
Chicago, IL	Apr 19	Oct 28	Milwaukee, WI	Apr 20	Oct 25
Cleveland, OH	Apr 21	Nov 2	Minneapolis, MN	Apr 30	Oct 13
Concord, NH	May 11	Sept 30	Montgomery, AL	Feb 27	Dec 3
Dallas, TX	Mar 18	Nov 17	Nashville, TN	Mar 28	Nov 7
Denver, CO	Apr 26	Oct 14	New Orleans, LA	Feb 20	Dec 9
Des Moines, IA	Apr 24	Oct 16	New York City, NY	Apr 7	Nov 12
Detroit, MI	Apr 21	Oct 20	Norfolk, VA	Mar 19	Nov 16

Plant Hardiness
Last & First Frost Dates

Average Frost Dates For United States

City	Last Spring Frost	First Fall Frost	City	Last Spring Frost	First Fall Frost
Okla City, OK	Mar 28	Nov 7	Springfield, IL	Apr 20	Oct 23
Omaha, NE	Apr 14	Oct 20	Springfield, MO	Apr 12	Oct 30
Philadelphia, PA	Mar 30	Nov 17	Syracuse, NY	Apr 30	Oct 15
Phoenix, AZ	Feb 5	Dec 6	Tampa, FL	Jan 10	Dec 26
Pittsburgh, PA	Apr 20	Oct 23	Texarkana, AR	Mar 21	Nov 9
Pocatello, ID	Apr 20	Oct 26	Trenton, NJ	Apr 4	Nov 8
Portland, ME	Apr 29	Oct 15	Tucson, AZ	Mar 19	Nov 19
Portland, OR	Mar 6	Nov 24	Washington, DC	Mar 29	Nov 9
Providence, RI	Apr 13	Oct 27	Wichita, KS	Apr 5	Nov 1
Pueblo, CO	Apr 23	Oct 14	Wilmington, DE	Apr 18	Oct 26
Raleigh, NC	Mar 24	Nov 16			
Rapid City, SD	May 7	Oct 4			
Reno, NV	May 8	Oct 10			
Richmond, VA	Mar 29	Nov 2			
Salt Lake City, UT	Apr 13	Oct 22			
San Francisco, CA	Jan 7	Dec 23			
Santa Fe, NM	Apr 24	Oct 19			
Savannah, GA	Feb 27	Nov 29			
Seattle, WA	Mar 14	Nov 24			
Shreveport, LA	Mar 8	Nov 15			
Sioux City, IA	Apr 27	Oct 13			
Sioux Falls, SD	May 5	Oct 3			

Notes

Canada Plant Hardiness Zone Map

Canada's plant hardiness map provides insights about what can grow where. It combines information about a variety of climatic conditions across the entire country to produce a single map. For more info **http://planthardiness.gc.ca**

Notes

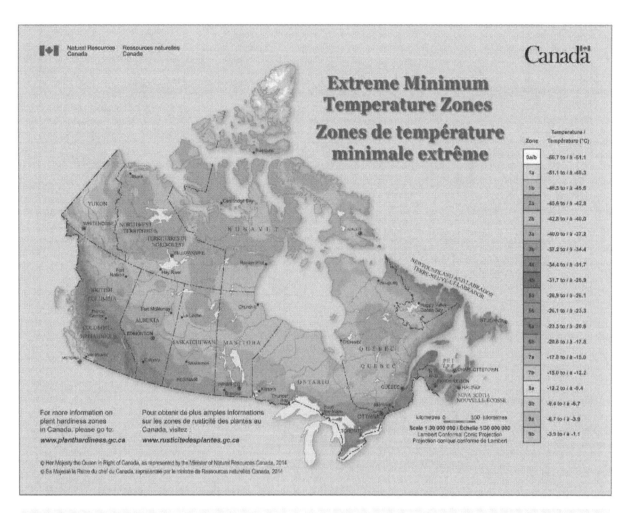

Plant hardiness zones for Canada based on the USDA extreme minimum temperature approach. For more info **http://planthardiness.gc.ca**

Notes

Plant Hardiness
Last & First Frost Dates

Average Frost Dates For Canada

City	Last Spring Frost	First Fall Frost
Vancouver, BC	Mar 31	Nov 3
Yellowknife, NWT	May 27	Sept 16
Whitehorse, YT	June 8	Aug 30
Calgary, AB	May 25	Sept 15
Edmonton, AB	May 6	Sept 24
Regina, SK	May 24	Sept 11
Winnipeg, MB	May 23	Sept 22
Kingston, ON	May 7	Oct 10
Niagara Falls, ON	May 3	Oct 23
Ottawa, ON	May 8	Sept 30
Sault Ste. Marie, ON	May 24	Sept 29
Sudbury, ON	May 12	Oct 2
Timmins, ON	May 28	Sept 13
Toronto, ON	April 20	Oct 29
Thunder Bay, ON	May 30	Sept 12
Windsor, ON	April 26	Oct 21
Montreal, PQ	April 19	Oct 14
Quebec City, PQ	May 10	Oct 15
Saint John, NB	May 2	Oct 21
Halifax, NS	Apr 30	Oct 19
Charlottetown, PE	May 16	Oct 14
St. John's, NF	June 1	Oct 11

Supplier Contact List

Company Name:	Street:	Notes:
Website:	City:	
Email:	State: Zip:	
Contact Name:	Products:	
Office Phone:		
Cell Phone:		

Company Name:	Street:	Notes:
Website:	City:	
Email:	State: Zip:	
Contact Name:	Products:	
Office Phone:		
Cell Phone:		

Company Name:	Street:	Notes:
Website:	City:	
Email:	State: Zip:	
Contact Name:	Products:	
Office Phone:		
Cell Phone:		

Company Name:	Street:	Notes:
Website:	City:	
Email:	State: Zip:	
Contact Name:	Products:	
Office Phone:		
Cell Phone:		

Company Name:	Street:	Notes:
Website:	City:	
Email:	State: Zip:	
Contact Name:	Products:	
Office Phone:		
Cell Phone:		

Supplier Contact List

Company Name:	Street:	Notes:
Website:	City:	
Email:	State: Zip:	
Contact Name:	Products:	
Office Phone:		
Cell Phone:		
Company Name:	Street:	Notes:
Website:	City:	
Email:	State: Zip:	
Contact Name:	Products:	
Office Phone:		
Cell Phone:		
Company Name:	Street:	Notes:
Website:	City:	
Email:	State: Zip:	
Contact Name:	Products:	
Office Phone:		
Cell Phone:		
Company Name:	Street:	Notes:
Website:	City:	
Email:	State: Zip:	
Contact Name:	Products:	
Office Phone:		
Cell Phone:		
Company Name:	Street:	Notes:
Website:	City:	
Email:	State: Zip:	
Contact Name:	Products:	
Office Phone:		
Cell Phone:		

Supplier Contact List

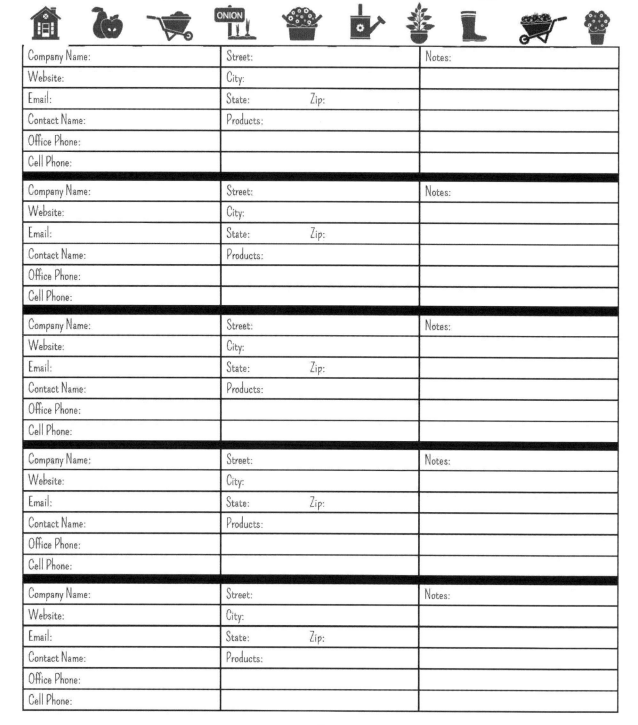

Company Name:	Street:	Notes:
Website:	City:	
Email:	State: Zip:	
Contact Name:	Products:	
Office Phone:		
Cell Phone:		

Company Name:	Street:	Notes:
Website:	City:	
Email:	State: Zip:	
Contact Name:	Products:	
Office Phone:		
Cell Phone:		

Company Name:	Street:	Notes:
Website:	City:	
Email:	State: Zip:	
Contact Name:	Products:	
Office Phone:		
Cell Phone:		

Company Name:	Street:	Notes:
Website:	City:	
Email:	State: Zip:	
Contact Name:	Products:	
Office Phone:		
Cell Phone:		

Company Name:	Street:	Notes:
Website:	City:	
Email:	State: Zip:	
Contact Name:	Products:	
Office Phone:		
Cell Phone:		

Seed Catologs To Order

Year: _____

Catalog	Comany	Website	Ordered
_____	_____	_____	☐
_____	_____	_____	☐
_____	_____	_____	☐
_____	_____	_____	☐
_____	_____	_____	☐
_____	_____	_____	☐
_____	_____	_____	☐
_____	_____	_____	☐
_____	_____	_____	☐
_____	_____	_____	☐
_____	_____	_____	☐
_____	_____	_____	☐
_____	_____	_____	☐
_____	_____	_____	☐
_____	_____	_____	☐

Notes:

Notes:

Seed Inventory

Year: _____

Plant Type	Brand	Variety	Used
_____	_____	_____	☐
_____	_____	_____	☐
_____	_____	_____	☐
_____	_____	_____	☐
_____	_____	_____	☐
_____	_____	_____	☐
_____	_____	_____	☐
_____	_____	_____	☐
_____	_____	_____	☐
_____	_____	_____	☐
_____	_____	_____	☐
_____	_____	_____	☐
_____	_____	_____	☐
_____	_____	_____	☐

Notes:

Notes:

Seed Inventory

Year: _____

Plant Type	Brand	Variety	Used
			☐
			☐
			☐
			☐
			☐
			☐
			☐
			☐
			☐
			☐
			☐
			☐
			☐
			☐

Notes:

Notes:

Seed Inventory

Year: _____

Plant Type	Brand	Variety	Used
_____	_____	_____	☐
_____	_____	_____	☐
_____	_____	_____	☐
_____	_____	_____	☐
_____	_____	_____	☐
_____	_____	_____	☐
_____	_____	_____	☐
_____	_____	_____	☐
_____	_____	_____	☐
_____	_____	_____	☐
_____	_____	_____	☐
_____	_____	_____	☐
_____	_____	_____	☐
_____	_____	_____	☐

Notes:

Notes:

Garden Budget Planner

YEAR: _____

VEGETABLES	AMOUNT:
SUBTOTAL:	

FERTILIZER/MISC	AMOUNT:
SUBTOTAL:	

FRUIT	AMOUNT:
SUBTOTAL:	

FLOWERS	AMOUNT:
SUBTOTAL:	

TOTALS	AMOUNT:
TOTAL:	

19

Gardening Expenses

ITEM#	DESCRIPTION	QTY	PRICE		NOTES
		TOTAL EXPENSES			

Plant
SEEDS OF
love

Welcome to my Garden

Garden Wish List

Notes:

Notes:

Herb Garden Wish List

_____

_____

_____

_____

_____

_____

_____

_____

_____

_____

_____

_____

_____

_____

_____

_____

Notes:

Notes:

Annual Flower Wish List

Seed	Source	Price	Bought
			☐
			☐
			☐
			☐
			☐
			☐
			☐
			☐
			☐
			☐
			☐
			☐
			☐
			☐
			☐
			☐

Notes:

Notes:

Seed Wish List

Seed	Source	Price	Bought
			☐
			☐
			☐
			☐
			☐
			☐
			☐
			☐
			☐
			☐
			☐
			☐
			☐
			☐
			☐
			☐

Notes:

Notes:

Tree Wish List

Seed	Source	Price	Bought
_____	_____	_____	☐
_____	_____	_____	☐
_____	_____	_____	☐
_____	_____	_____	☐
_____	_____	_____	☐
_____	_____	_____	☐
_____	_____	_____	☐
_____	_____	_____	☐
_____	_____	_____	☐
_____	_____	_____	☐
_____	_____	_____	☐
_____	_____	_____	☐
_____	_____	_____	☐
_____	_____	_____	☐
_____	_____	_____	☐

Notes:

Notes:

Herb Seed & Plant Wish List

Seed & Plant	Source	Price	Bought
			☐
			☐
			☐
			☐
			☐
			☐
			☐
			☐
			☐
			☐
			☐
			☐
			☐
			☐
			☐
			☐

Notes:

Notes:

Fruit Wish List

Seed	Source	Price	Bought
			☐
			☐
			☐
			☐
			☐
			☐
			☐
			☐
			☐
			☐
			☐
			☐
			☐
			☐
			☐
			☐

Notes: Notes:

Perenial Flower Wish List

Seed	Source	Price	Bought
_____	_____	_____	☐
_____	_____	_____	☐
_____	_____	_____	☐
_____	_____	_____	☐
_____	_____	_____	☐
_____	_____	_____	☐
_____	_____	_____	☐
_____	_____	_____	☐
_____	_____	_____	☐
_____	_____	_____	☐
_____	_____	_____	☐
_____	_____	_____	☐
_____	_____	_____	☐
_____	_____	_____	☐
_____	_____	_____	☐
_____	_____	_____	☐

Notes:

Notes:

Plant Wish List

Seed	Source	Price	Bought
			☐
			☐
			☐
			☐
			☐
			☐
			☐
			☐
			☐
			☐
			☐
			☐
			☐
			☐
			☐
			☐
			☐

Notes:

Notes:

Garden Plant Wish List

_____

_____

_____

_____

_____

_____

_____

_____

_____

_____

_____

_____

_____

Notes:

Notes:

Tool Log

Tool Log

_____   _____
_____   _____
_____   _____
_____   _____
_____   _____
_____   _____
_____   _____
_____   _____
_____   _____
_____   _____
_____   _____
_____   _____
_____   _____
_____   _____
_____   _____
_____   _____

Tool Wish List

Tool	Source	Price	Bought
			☐
			☐
			☐
			☐
			☐
			☐
			☐
			☐
			☐
			☐
			☐
			☐
			☐
			☐
			☐
			☐

Plant SEEDS OF friendship

GARDEN LAYOUT

Welcome to my Garden

Plot Design

_____

Spring Garden Plan

Assign each plant a letter and fill in the grid below to map out your Spring Garden

A	B	C	D	E	F	G
H	I	J	K	L	M	N
O	P	Q	R	S	T	U
V	W	X	Y	Z		

Summer Garden Plan

Assign each plant a letter and fill in the grid below to map out your Summer Garden

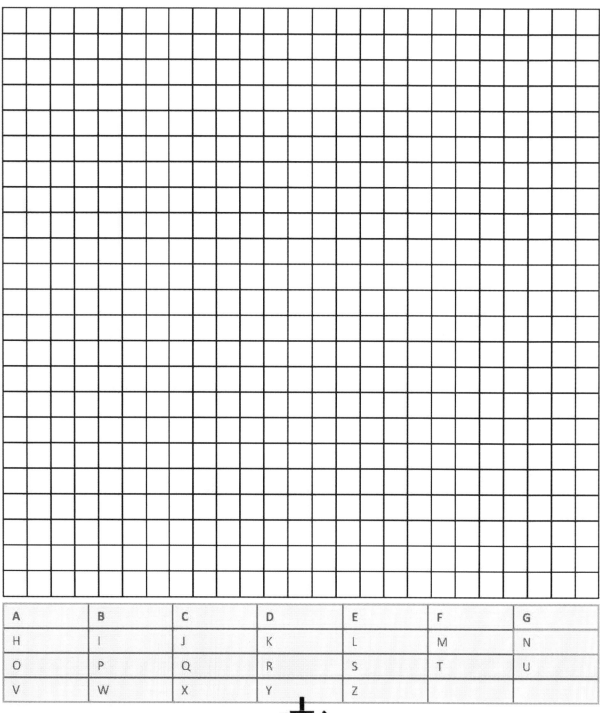

A	B	C	D	E	F	G
H	I	J	K	L	M	N
O	P	Q	R	S	T	U
V	W	X	Y	Z		

Autumn Garden Planner

Assign each plant a letter and fill in the grid below to map out your Autumn Garden

A	B	C	D	E	F	G
H	I	J	K	L	M	N
O	P	Q	R	S	T	U
V	W	X	Y	Z		

Winter Garden Plan

Assign each plant a letter and fill in the grid below to map out your Winter Garden

A	B	C	D	E	F	G
H	I	J	K	L	M	N
O	P	Q	R	S	T	U
V	W	X	Y	Z		

Garden Notes

Notes:

Notes:

Garden Layout Plan

Year_____

Key To Garden
Layout:

_____

_____

_____

_____

_____

_____

_____

_____

_____

_____

_____

Garden Layout Plan

Garden Layout Plan

Year_____

Key To Garden
Layout:

_____

_____

_____

_____

_____

_____

_____

_____

_____

_____

Garden Layout Plan

Garden Pictures

Garden Pictures

Plant SEEDS OF friendship

GARDEN FORMS

Welcome to my Garden

GARDENING  CALENDAR

January

Protect your garden from frosts, winds and rain. Start planning garden plot for the next year.

February

Trim bushes and evergreen hedges. Prepare seed beds. Chit potato tubers.

March

Sow seeds. Trim winter shrubs. Clean up around the garden. Plant shallots, onion sets, early potatoes, summer-flowering bulbs.

April

Finish any digging. Start sowing outdoors. Sow hardy annuals and herb seeds. Watch out for late frosts.

May

Sow and plant out bedding. Earth up potatoes. Plant out summer bedding. Mow lawns weekly.

June

Hoe weeds regularly. Sow Beans. Water trees. Harvest lettuce, radish, other salads and early potatoes

July

Water tubs and new plants. Deadhead bedding plants. Harvest zucchini.

August

Water your garden. Prune summer-flowering bushes. Collect seeds. Harvest sweetcorn and other vegetables

September

Harvest fruits and vegetables. Pot up herbs. Sow broad beans and hardy peas. Plant spring flowering bulbs.

October

Clear up fallen leaves. Move tender plants into the greenhouse. Plant out spring cabbages.

November

Start a new compost heap. Plant tulip bulbs. Plant out winter bedding. Prune roses.

December

Check garden winter protection. Prune apples and pears. Take hardwood cuttings.

Gardening Projects

YEARLY GOALS

NEW PROJECTS

TECHNIQUES

NOTES

YEAR AT A GLANCE

I'M A
Nature Addict

MEDITATING

Mud Playin'

GARDENING

kinda girl!

Welcome to my Garden

At-a-Glance Year Planner

	Job 1	Job 2	Job 3	Job 4	Job 5
January					
February					
March					
April					
May					
June					
July					
August					
Sept.					
Oct.					
Nov.					
Dec.					

Seed Starter Log

Year: _____

Date	Plant	When to Transplant	Done
_____	_____	_____	☐
_____	_____	_____	☐
_____	_____	_____	☐
_____	_____	_____	☐
_____	_____	_____	☐
_____	_____	_____	☐
_____	_____	_____	☐
_____	_____	_____	☐
_____	_____	_____	☐
_____	_____	_____	☐
_____	_____	_____	☐
_____	_____	_____	☐
_____	_____	_____	☐
_____	_____	_____	☐
_____	_____	_____	☐

Notes:

Notes:

Seed Starter Log

Year: _____

Date	Plant	When to Transplant	Done
_____	_____	_____	☐
_____	_____	_____	☐
_____	_____	_____	☐
_____	_____	_____	☐
_____	_____	_____	☐
_____	_____	_____	☐
_____	_____	_____	☐
_____	_____	_____	☐
_____	_____	_____	☐
_____	_____	_____	☐
_____	_____	_____	☐
_____	_____	_____	☐
_____	_____	_____	☐
_____	_____	_____	☐

Notes:

Notes:

Seed Starter Log
Year: _____

Date	Plant	When to Transplant	Done
_____	_____	_____	☐
_____	_____	_____	☐
_____	_____	_____	☐
_____	_____	_____	☐
_____	_____	_____	☐
_____	_____	_____	☐
_____	_____	_____	☐
_____	_____	_____	☐
_____	_____	_____	☐
_____	_____	_____	☐
_____	_____	_____	☐
_____	_____	_____	☐
_____	_____	_____	☐
_____	_____	_____	☐

Notes:

Notes:

Transplanting Schedule

Date   Plant   Location   Planted

☐
☐
☐
☐
☐
☐
☐
☐
☐
☐
☐
☐
☐
☐
☐
☐
☐
☐
☐
☐
☐
☐
☐
☐

Vegetables Planting Tracker

Herb Plant	Date Planted	Expected Harvest Date	Yield	Observations and Notes

Herbs Planting Tracker

Herb Plant	Date Planted	Expected Harvest Date	Yield	Observations and Notes

Flower Planting Tracker

Plant	Date Planted	Expected Bloom	Observations and Notes

Potted Plant Planner

Plant	Date Potted	Expected Bloom	Observations and Notes

Monthly Harvest Calendar

Month:

Month:

Month:

Month:

Month:

Month:

Month:

Month:

Month:

Master To-Do List

To Do   Done

☐
☐
☐
☐
☐
☐
☐
☐
☐
☐
☐
☐
☐
☐
☐
☐
☐
☐
☐
☐
☐
☐
☐

Yearly Tasks

Date	To Do	Done
_____	_____	☐
_____	_____	☐
_____	_____	☐
_____	_____	☐
_____	_____	☐
_____	_____	☐
_____	_____	☐
_____	_____	☐
_____	_____	☐
_____	_____	☐
_____	_____	☐
_____	_____	☐
_____	_____	☐
_____	_____	☐

Notes:

Monthly Tasks

Date	To Do	Done
_____	_____	☐
_____	_____	☐
_____	_____	☐
_____	_____	☐
_____	_____	☐
_____	_____	☐
_____	_____	☐
_____	_____	☐
_____	_____	☐
_____	_____	☐
_____	_____	☐
_____	_____	☐
_____	_____	☐
_____	_____	☐

Notes:

Weekly Tasks

Date	To Do	Done
_____	_____	☐
_____	_____	☐
_____	_____	☐
_____	_____	☐
_____	_____	☐
_____	_____	☐
_____	_____	☐
_____	_____	☐
_____	_____	☐
_____	_____	☐
_____	_____	☐
_____	_____	☐
_____	_____	☐
_____	_____	☐

Notes:

Daily Tasks

Date	To Do	Done
_____	_____	☐
_____	_____	☐
_____	_____	☐
_____	_____	☐
_____	_____	☐
_____	_____	☐
_____	_____	☐
_____	_____	☐
_____	_____	☐
_____	_____	☐
_____	_____	☐
_____	_____	☐
_____	_____	☐
_____	_____	☐

Notes:

Garden Notes

Notes:

Notes:

Garden Notes

Notes:

Notes:

MONTHLY JOURNAL

Welcome to my Garden

Seasonal Notes

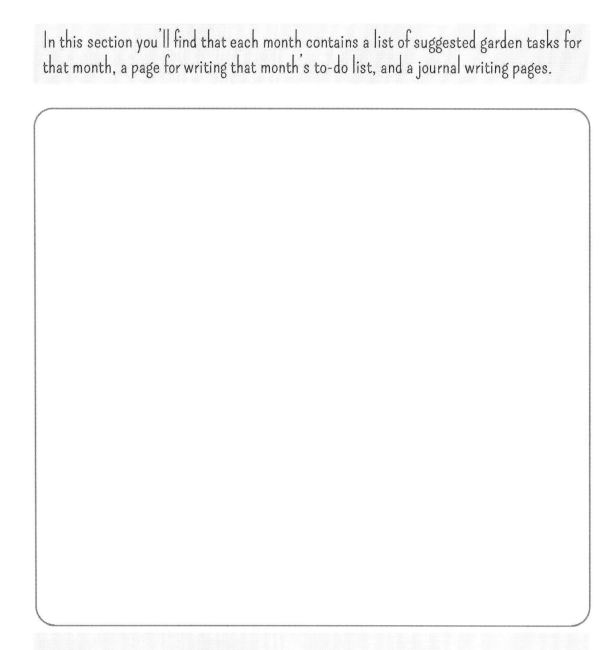

In this section you'll find that each month contains a list of suggested garden tasks for that month, a page for writing that month's to-do list, and a journal writing pages.

Remember that children, marriages, and flower gardens reflect the kind of care they get.
H. Jackson Brown, Jr.

Seasonal Tasks

Date	To Do	Done
_____	_____	☐
_____	_____	☐
_____	_____	☐
_____	_____	☐
_____	_____	☐
_____	_____	☐
_____	_____	☐
_____	_____	☐
_____	_____	☐
_____	_____	☐
_____	_____	☐
_____	_____	☐
_____	_____	☐
_____	_____	☐

Notes:

Seasonal To Do List

SPRING

- [ ]
- [ ]
- [ ]
- [ ]
- [ ]
- [ ]
- [ ]
- [ ]

SUMMER

- [ ]
- [ ]
- [ ]
- [ ]
- [ ]
- [ ]
- [ ]
- [ ]

FALL

- [ ]
- [ ]
- [ ]
- [ ]
- [ ]
- [ ]
- [ ]
- [ ]

WINTER

- [ ]
- [ ]
- [ ]
- [ ]
- [ ]
- [ ]
- [ ]
- [ ]

Notes

Things To Remember For Next Year

DATE_____

Garden Notes

Notes:

Notes:

Garden Notes

Notes:

Notes:

JANUARY

MY
garden
IS MY
HAPPY PLACE

Welcome to my Garden

January

Sun	Mon	Tues	Wed	Thurs	Fri	Sat

Important Notes & Reminders

_____

_____

_____

Goals For The Month Of January

Garden

- _____
- _____
- _____
- _____
- _____

Herbs

- _____
- _____
- _____
- _____
- _____

Family

- _____
- _____
- _____
- _____
- _____

Home

- _____
- _____
- _____
- _____
- _____

Clean It Up

- _____
- _____
- _____
- _____
- _____

Rewards

- _____
- _____
- _____
- _____
- _____

Health

- _____
- _____
- _____
- _____
- _____

Best Things That Happened!

_____

_____

_____

_____

_____

January Garden Tips, Projects & Goals

Garden Tips

Put your live Christmas tree in a pond or creek for little fish to live in.

Plant your Live Christmas tree outside.

Water and fertilize poinsettias and Christmas cactuses.

Force early flowering trees and shrubs to bloom inside.

Put on your thinking cap and draw out your veggie garden and herb garden for the coming season.

Start your Garden Notes Page in the back of this journal, keeping notes all year long. Temperatures, First Frosts, Harvesting notes, etc.

Personal Projects

- ❑ _____
- ❑ _____
- ❑ _____
- ❑ _____
- ❑ _____
- ❑ _____
- ❑ _____
- ❑ _____
- ❑ _____
- ❑ _____
- ❑ _____
- ❑ _____
- ❑ _____

Garden Projects

- ❑ _____
- ❑ _____
- ❑ _____
- ❑ _____
- ❑ _____
- ❑ _____
- ❑ _____
- ❑ _____
- ❑ _____
- ❑ _____
- ❑ _____
- ❑ _____
- ❑ _____

I'm Grateful For:

 Month: _____

Weather

_____
_____
_____
_____
_____
_____

Sow	Plant	Harvest	Feed
_____	_____	_____	_____
_____	_____	_____	_____
_____	_____	_____	_____
_____	_____	_____	_____
_____	_____	_____	_____

Prune

_____
_____
_____
_____

Every gardener knows that under the cloak of winter lies a miracle.
Luther Burbank

JOB 1

Notes:

Notes:

 JOB 2

Notes:

Notes:

JOB 3

Notes:

Notes:

JOB 4

Notes:

Notes:

JOB 5

Notes:

Notes:

Garden Notes

Notes:

Notes:

Garden Notes

Notes:

Notes:

FEBRUARY

I LOVE TO PLAY IN THE dirt

Welcome to my Garden

February

Sun	Mon	Tues	Wed	Thurs	Fri	Sat

Important Notes & Reminders

_____

_____

_____

_____

Goals For The Month Of February

Garden

- _____
- _____
- _____
- _____
- _____

Herbs

- _____
- _____
- _____
- _____
- _____

Family

- _____
- _____
- _____
- _____
- _____

Home

- _____
- _____
- _____
- _____
- _____

Clean It Up

- _____
- _____
- _____
- _____
- _____

Rewards

- _____
- _____
- _____
- _____
- _____

Health

- _____
- _____
- _____
- _____
- _____

Best Things That Happened!

_____

_____

_____

_____

_____

February Garden Tips, Projects & Goals

Garden Tips

Order seeds from Catalogs.

Preserve any Flowers you get for Valentines day to make potpourris and save citrus peelings too.

Fertilize Fruit Trees.

Start early seeds indoors, like broccoli, cabbage and cauliflower.

Prune grapes and clean out raspberry bushes of dead limbs.

Plant Snow peas.

Take cuttings from Scented Geraniums. They make perfect house plants and they thrive outdoors in the garden or in pots. Easy to take cuttings to share with your friends. They smell so good!

Personal Projects

- ❑ _____
- ❑ _____
- ❑ _____
- ❑ _____
- ❑ _____
- ❑ _____
- ❑ _____
- ❑ _____
- ❑ _____
- ❑ _____
- ❑ _____
- ❑ _____
- ❑ _____

Garden Projects

- ❑ _____
- ❑ _____
- ❑ _____
- ❑ _____
- ❑ _____
- ❑ _____
- ❑ _____
- ❑ _____
- ❑ _____
- ❑ _____
- ❑ _____
- ❑ _____
- ❑ _____

I'm Grateful For:

Month: _____

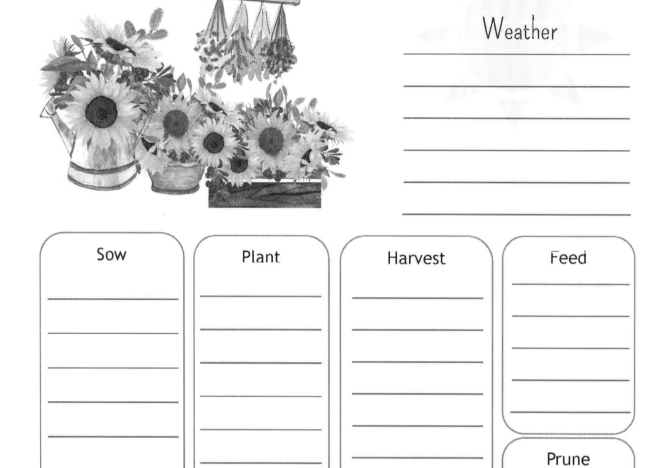

Weather
_____
_____
_____
_____
_____
_____

Sow	Plant	Harvest	Feed

Prune

A garden is a grand teacher. It teaches patience and careful watchfulness; it teaches industry and thrift; above all it teaches entire trust.
Gertrude Jekyll

JOB 1

Notes:

Notes:

JOB 2

Notes:

Notes:

JOB 3

Notes:

Notes:

JOB 4

Notes:

Notes:

JOB 5

Notes:

Notes:

Garden Notes

_____

_____

_____

_____

_____

_____

_____

_____

_____

_____

_____

_____

_____

_____

Notes: Notes:

SPRING

Plant SEEDS OF friendship

Welcome to my Garden

Spring Tasks

Date	To Do	Done
_____	_____	☐
_____	_____	☐
_____	_____	☐
_____	_____	☐
_____	_____	☐
_____	_____	☐
_____	_____	☐
_____	_____	☐
_____	_____	☐
_____	_____	☐
_____	_____	☐
_____	_____	☐
_____	_____	☐
_____	_____	☐

Notes:

Spring Tasks

Date	To Do	Done
_____	_____	☐
_____	_____	☐
_____	_____	☐
_____	_____	☐
_____	_____	☐
_____	_____	☐
_____	_____	☐
_____	_____	☐
_____	_____	☐
_____	_____	☐
_____	_____	☐
_____	_____	☐
_____	_____	☐
_____	_____	☐

Notes:

MARCH

My
garden
IS MY
HAPPY PLACE

Welcome to my Garden

March

Sun	Mon	Tues	Wed	Thurs	Fri	Sat

Important Notes & Reminders

_____

_____

_____

Goals For The Month Of March

Garden

- —————————
- —————————
- —————————
- —————————
- —————————

Herbs

- —————————
- —————————
- —————————
- —————————
- —————————

Family

- —————————
- —————————
- —————————
- —————————
- —————————

Home

- —————————
- —————————
- —————————
- —————————
- —————————

Clean It Up

- —————————
- —————————
- —————————
- —————————
- —————————

Rewards

- —————————
- —————————
- —————————
- —————————
- —————————

Health

- —————————
- —————————
- —————————
- —————————
- —————————

Best Things That Happened!

—————————————————
—————————————————
—————————————————
—————————————————

March Garden Tips, Projects & Goals

Garden Tips

Bring in Forsythia and Pussy Willow inside to force bloom.

Plan out Veggie Garden and Herb Garden in your Garden Notebook.

Get Little Garden Spot ready for Salad, prepare soil for it.

Plant rhubarb.

Plant Cold Season Crops, snow peas, lettuce. Broccoli and Cauliflower.

Divide Perennials and Plant new ones.

Start Herb Seeds indoors.

Personal Projects

☐ _____
☐ _____
☐ _____
☐ _____
☐ _____
☐ _____
☐ _____
☐ _____
☐ _____
☐ _____
☐ _____
☐ _____
☐ _____

Garden Projects

☐ _____
☐ _____
☐ _____
☐ _____
☐ _____
☐ _____
☐ _____
☐ _____
☐ _____
☐ _____
☐ _____
☐ _____
☐ _____

I'm Grateful For:

 Month: _____

Weather
_____
_____
_____
_____
_____
_____

Sow	Plant	Harvest	Feed

Prune

In the spring, at the end of the day, you should smell like dirt.
Margaret Atwood

JOB 1

_____
_____
_____
_____
_____
_____
_____
_____
_____
_____
_____
_____
_____
_____
_____
_____

Notes: Notes:

JOB 2

Notes:

Notes:

JOB 3

_____

_____

_____

_____

_____

_____

_____

_____

_____

_____

_____

_____

_____

_____

_____

_____

Notes:

Notes:

JOB 4

Notes:

Notes:

JOB 5

Notes:

Notes:

Garden Notes

Notes:

Notes:

Garden Notes

Notes:

Notes:

APRIL

April
SHOWERS
bring MAY
flowers

Welcome to my Garden

April

Sun	Mon	Tues	Wed	Thurs	Fri	Sat

Important Notes & Reminders

_____

_____

_____

Goals For The Month Of April

Garden

- _____
- _____
- _____
- _____
- _____

Herbs

- _____
- _____
- _____
- _____
- _____

Family

- _____
- _____
- _____
- _____
- _____

Home

- _____
- _____
- _____
- _____
- _____

Clean It Up

- _____
- _____
- _____
- _____
- _____

Rewards

- _____
- _____
- _____
- _____
- _____

Health

- _____
- _____
- _____
- _____
- _____

Best Things That Happened!

_____

_____

_____

_____

April Garden Tips, Projects & Goals

Garden Tips	Personal Projects	Garden Projects
Start Warm Weather Seeds Inside.	❑ _____	❑ _____
Start Warm Weather Seeds Inside.	❑ _____	❑ _____
	❑ _____	❑ _____
Plant Carrots and Radishes.	❑ _____	❑ _____
	❑ _____	❑ _____
Plant New Trees.	❑ _____	❑ _____
	❑ _____	❑ _____
	❑ _____	❑ _____
Plant Snap peas and Lima Beans.	❑ _____	❑ _____
	❑ _____	❑ _____
Prune Peach Trees.	❑ _____	❑ _____
	❑ _____	❑ _____
Check Trees for Carpet Worms. Clean out Herb Garden Bed of all Dead Growth. And pull up any wondering herbs, like mint or Lemon Balm. Share with a friend.		

I'm Grateful For:

Month:

Weather
_____
_____
_____
_____
_____
_____

Sow	Plant	Harvest	Feed
_____	_____	_____	_____
_____	_____	_____	_____
_____	_____	_____	_____
_____	_____	_____	_____
_____	_____	_____	_____
_____	_____	_____	

Prune
_____
_____
_____
_____
_____

A garden always gives back more than it receives.
National Garden Bureau

JOB 1

_____

_____

_____

_____

_____

_____

_____

_____

_____

_____

_____

_____

_____

Notes:

Notes:

JOB 2

Notes:

Notes:

JOB 3

_____

_____

_____

_____

_____

_____

_____

_____

_____

_____

_____

_____

_____

_____

_____

Notes:

Notes:

JOB 4

Notes:

Notes:

JOB 5

Notes:

Notes:

Garden Notes

Notes:

Notes:

Garden Notes

Notes:

Notes:

MAY

One

WHO PLANTS A GARDEN
PLANTS HAPPINESS

Welcome to my Garden

May

Sun	Mon	Tues	Wed	Thurs	Fri	Sat

Important Notes & Reminders

_____

_____

_____

Goals For The Month Of May

Garden

- _____
- _____
- _____
- _____
- _____

Herbs

- _____
- _____
- _____
- _____
- _____

Family

- _____
- _____
- _____
- _____
- _____

Home

- _____
- _____
- _____
- _____
- _____

Clean It Up

- _____
- _____
- _____
- _____
- _____

Rewards

- _____
- _____
- _____
- _____
- _____

Health

- _____
- _____
- _____
- _____
- _____

Best Things That Happened!

_____

_____

_____

_____

_____

May Garden Tips, Projects & Goals

Garden Tips

Prune Evergreens.

Move house plants outdoors.

Buy and Plant Tomato Plants, smaller the better.

Plant a Luffa Gourd Seeds.
Plant corn.

Thin Bedding Flowers, Carrots, Beets, Lettuce, onions, radishes and spinach.
Pick Strawberries

Transplant Seeds you grew into the garden or Herb garden.

Plant Bush Basil around patio to dispel flies.

Personal Projects

☐ _____
☐ _____
☐ _____
☐ _____
☐ _____
☐ _____
☐ _____
☐ _____
☐ _____
☐ _____
☐ _____
☐ _____
☐ _____

Garden Projects

☐ _____
☐ _____
☐ _____
☐ _____
☐ _____
☐ _____
☐ _____
☐ _____
☐ _____
☐ _____
☐ _____
☐ _____
☐ _____

I'm Grateful For:

 Month: _____

Weather
_____
_____
_____
_____
_____
_____

Sow	Plant	Harvest	Feed

Prune

A The love of gardening is a seed once sown that never dies.
Gertrude Jekyll

JOB 1

Notes:

Notes:

JOB 2

Notes:

Notes:

JOB 3

_____

_____

_____

_____

_____

_____

_____

_____

_____

_____

_____

_____

_____

_____

_____

Notes:

Notes:

JOB 4

Notes:

Notes:

JOB 5

Notes:

Notes:

SUMMER

welcome
SUMMER

Welcome to my Garden

Summer Tasks

Date	To Do	Done
_____	_____	☐
_____	_____	☐
_____	_____	☐
_____	_____	☐
_____	_____	☐
_____	_____	☐
_____	_____	☐
_____	_____	☐
_____	_____	☐
_____	_____	☐
_____	_____	☐
_____	_____	☐
_____	_____	☐
_____	_____	☐

Notes:

Summer Tasks

Date	To Do	Done
_____	_____	☐
_____	_____	☐
_____	_____	☐
_____	_____	☐
_____	_____	☐
_____	_____	☐
_____	_____	☐
_____	_____	☐
_____	_____	☐
_____	_____	☐
_____	_____	☐
_____	_____	☐
_____	_____	☐
_____	_____	☐

Notes:

Garden Notes

Notes:

Notes:

JUNE

Gardening
IS CHEAPER
THAN THERAPY

Welcome to my Garden

June

Sun	Mon	Tues	Wed	Thurs	Fri	Sat

Important Notes & Reminders

Goals For The Month Of June

Garden

- _____
- _____
- _____
- _____
- _____

Herbs

- _____
- _____
- _____
- _____
- _____

Family

- _____
- _____
- _____
- _____
- _____

Home

- _____
- _____
- _____
- _____
- _____

Clean It Up

- _____
- _____
- _____
- _____
- _____

Rewards

- _____
- _____
- _____
- _____
- _____

Health

- _____
- _____
- _____
- _____
- _____

Best Things That Happened!

_____
_____
_____
_____
_____

June Garden Tips, Projects & Goals

Garden Tips	Personal Projects	Garden Projects
Divide and Reset Irises.	❏ _____	❏ _____
	❏ _____	❏ _____
Set out Cannas, Caladiums and elephant ears.	❏ _____	❏ _____
	❏ _____	❏ _____
Fix up Strawberry Patch.	❏ _____	❏ _____
	❏ _____	❏ _____
Mulch Garden. Plant Halloween Pumpkins.	❏ _____	❏ _____
	❏ _____	❏ _____
Start Seeds For Fall Garden. Pick Raspberries.	❏ _____	❏ _____
	❏ _____	❏ _____
Take out Spinach, Radishes and lettuce and plant beans or corn in its place.	❏ _____	❏ _____
	❏ _____	❏ _____
Harvest Herbs Once a month until September.	❏ _____	❏ _____

I'm Grateful For:

 Month: _____

Weather
_____
_____
_____
_____
_____
_____

Sow	Plant	Harvest	Feed

Prune

To plant a garden is to believe in tomorrow
Audrey Hepburn

JOB 1

_____
_____
_____
_____
_____
_____
_____
_____
_____
_____
_____
_____
_____
_____
_____

Notes:

Notes:

JOB 2

Notes:

Notes:

JOB 3

Notes:

Notes:

JOB 4

Notes:

Notes:

JOB 5

_____

_____

_____

_____

_____

_____

_____

_____

_____

_____

_____

_____

_____

_____

Notes: Notes:

Garden Notes

Notes:

Notes:

Garden Notes

Notes:

Notes:

JULY

GARDEN as though YOU WILL LIVE forever

Welcome to my Garden

July

Sun	Mon	Tues	Wed	Thurs	Fri	Sat

Important Notes & Reminders

Goals For The Month Of July

Garden

- _____
- _____
- _____
- _____
- _____

Herbs

- _____
- _____
- _____
- _____
- _____

Family

- _____
- _____
- _____
- _____
- _____

Home

- _____
- _____
- _____
- _____
- _____

Clean It Up

- _____
- _____
- _____
- _____
- _____

Rewards

- _____
- _____
- _____
- _____
- _____

Health

- _____
- _____
- _____
- _____
- _____

Best Things That Happened!

_____
_____
_____
_____

July Garden Tips, Projects & Goals

Garden Tips

Pinch back, fertilize and mulch Mums.

Cut Flowers for inside bouquets.

Clean out garden and plant fall crops.

Dig and divide Iris.

Dig and divide Day Lilies.

Pick Summer Savory herbs to add to your Green Beans.

Make some Iced Mint Tea or Lemon Balm Tea.

Keep Basil from going to seed by pinching off seed heads regularly.

Personal Projects

- ☐ _____
- ☐ _____
- ☐ _____
- ☐ _____
- ☐ _____
- ☐ _____
- ☐ _____
- ☐ _____
- ☐ _____
- ☐ _____
- ☐ _____
- ☐ _____
- ☐ _____

Garden Projects

- ☐ _____
- ☐ _____
- ☐ _____
- ☐ _____
- ☐ _____
- ☐ _____
- ☐ _____
- ☐ _____
- ☐ _____
- ☐ _____
- ☐ _____
- ☐ _____
- ☐ _____

I'm Grateful For:

Month: _____

Weather
_____
_____
_____
_____
_____
_____

Sow	Plant	Harvest	Feed

Prune

A gardener learns more in the mistakes than in the successes.
Barbara Dodge Borland

JOB 1

Notes:

Notes:

JOB 2

_____

_____

_____

_____

_____

_____

_____

_____

_____

_____

_____

_____

_____

_____

Notes:

Notes:

JOB 3

Notes:

Notes:

JOB 4

_____
_____
_____
_____
_____
_____
_____
_____
_____
_____
_____
_____
_____
_____

Notes: Notes:

JOB 5

Notes:

Notes:

Garden Notes

Notes:

Notes:

Garden Notes

Notes:

Notes:

AUGUST

Let nature be in your YARD

Welcome to my Garden

August

Sun	Mon	Tues	Wed	Thurs	Fri	Sat

Important Notes & Reminders

_____

_____

_____

Goals For The Month Of August

Garden

- _____
- _____
- _____
- _____
- _____

Herbs

- _____
- _____
- _____
- _____
- _____

Family

- _____
- _____
- _____
- _____
- _____

Home

- _____
- _____
- _____
- _____
- _____

Clean It Up

- _____
- _____
- _____
- _____
- _____

Rewards

- _____
- _____
- _____
- _____
- _____

Health

- _____
- _____
- _____
- _____
- _____

Best Things That Happened!

_____
_____
_____
_____
_____

August Garden Tips, Projects & Goals

Garden Tips

Begin transforming Luffa gourd Into a sponge.

Harvest Grapes Two or Three weeks after color change.

Make a list of Bulbs to get to be planted in the fall.

Prune Raspberry and Blackberry canes that bore fruit.

Pick dead buds off plants to keep blooming.
Begin Fall Garden.

Take cuttings from scented geraniums, Lemon verbena and rosemary.

Place in moist soil in shady spot, make great indoor plants for winter.

Personal Projects

❑ _____
❑ _____
❑ _____
❑ _____
❑ _____
❑ _____
❑ _____
❑ _____
❑ _____
❑ _____
❑ _____
❑ _____
❑ _____

Garden Projects

❑ _____
❑ _____
❑ _____
❑ _____
❑ _____
❑ _____
❑ _____
❑ _____
❑ _____
❑ _____
❑ _____
❑ _____
❑ _____

I'm Grateful For:

JOB 1

Notes:

Notes:

JOB 2

Notes:

Notes:

JOB 3

_____

_____

_____

_____

_____

_____

_____

_____

_____

_____

_____

_____

_____

_____

_____

Notes:

Notes:

JOB 4

_____

_____

_____

_____

_____

_____

_____

_____

_____

_____

_____

_____

_____

_____

Notes:

Notes:

JOB 5

Notes:

Notes:

Garden Notes

Notes:

Notes:

Garden Notes

Notes:

Notes:

Autumn

Autumn leaves & pumpkins please

Welcome to my Garden

Autumn Tasks

Date	To Do	Done
_____	_____	☐
_____	_____	☐
_____	_____	☐
_____	_____	☐
_____	_____	☐
_____	_____	☐
_____	_____	☐
_____	_____	☐
_____	_____	☐
_____	_____	☐
_____	_____	☐
_____	_____	☐
_____	_____	☐
_____	_____	☐

Notes:

HAPPY FALL

Autumn Tasks

Date	To Do	Done
_____	_____	☐
_____	_____	☐
_____	_____	☐
_____	_____	☐
_____	_____	☐
_____	_____	☐
_____	_____	☐
_____	_____	☐
_____	_____	☐
_____	_____	☐
_____	_____	☐
_____	_____	☐
_____	_____	☐
_____	_____	☐

Notes:

SEPTEMBER

AN OPTIMISTIC gardener IS ONE who believes THAT WHATEVER GOES DOWN must come up

Welcome to my Garden

September

Sun	Mon	Tues	Wed	Thurs	Fri	Sat

Important Notes & Reminders

Goals For The Month Of September

Garden

- _____
- _____
- _____
- _____
- _____

Herbs

- _____
- _____
- _____
- _____
- _____

Family

- _____
- _____
- _____
- _____
- _____

Home

- _____
- _____
- _____
- _____
- _____

Clean It Up

- _____
- _____
- _____
- _____
- _____

Rewards

- _____
- _____
- _____
- _____
- _____

Health

- _____
- _____
- _____
- _____
- _____

Best Things That Happened!

_____

_____

_____

_____

_____

 Month: _____

Weather
_____
_____
_____
_____
_____
_____

Sow	Plant	Harvest	Feed

Prune

Gardens are not made by singing 'Oh, how beautiful,' and sitting in the shade.
Rudyard Kipling

September Garden Tips, Projects & Goals

Garden Tips

Get Christmas Cactuses Ready to Bloom.

Bring in houseplants.

Plant Parsley Seeds for indoor Growing.

Fertilize Strawberries.

Divide day lilies, iris, phlox and peonies.

Dig Potatoes.

Dig up and store cannas, dahlias, and geraniums.

Save flower seeds for next year.

Harvest Dill top half when seed heads are beige.

Personal Projects

❏ _____
❏ _____
❏ _____
❏ _____
❏ _____
❏ _____
❏ _____
❏ _____
❏ _____
❏ _____
❏ _____
❏ _____
❏ _____

Garden Projects

❏ _____
❏ _____
❏ _____
❏ _____
❏ _____
❏ _____
❏ _____
❏ _____
❏ _____
❏ _____
❏ _____
❏ _____
❏ _____

I'm Grateful For:

JOB 1

_____

_____

_____

_____

_____

_____

_____

_____

_____

_____

_____

_____

_____

Notes:

Notes:

JOB 2

Notes:

Notes:

JOB 3

Notes:

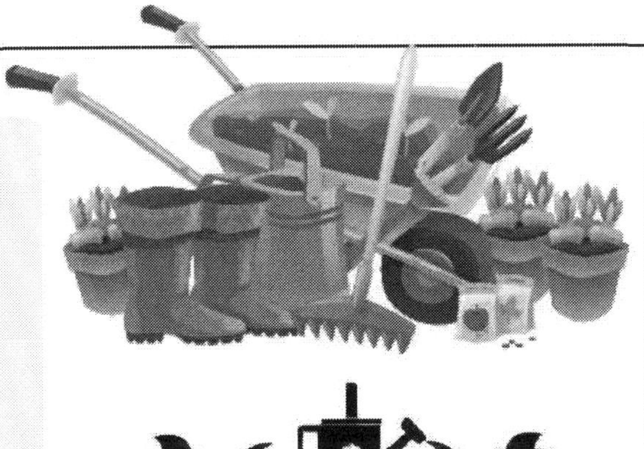

Notes:

JOB 4

Notes:

Notes:

JOB 5

Notes:

Notes:

Garden Notes

Notes:

Notes:

Garden Notes

Notes:

Notes:

OCTOBER

Fall is in the air...

Welcome to my Garden

October

Sun	Mon	Tues	Wed	Thurs	Fri	Sat

Important Notes & Reminders

_____

_____

_____

Goals For The Month Of October

Garden

- _____
- _____
- _____
- _____
- _____

Herbs

- _____
- _____
- _____
- _____
- _____

Family

- _____
- _____
- _____
- _____
- _____

Home

- _____
- _____
- _____
- _____
- _____

Clean It Up

- _____
- _____
- _____
- _____
- _____

Rewards

- _____
- _____
- _____
- _____
- _____

Health

- _____
- _____
- _____
- _____
- _____

Best Things That Happened!

_____
_____
_____
_____

October Garden Tips, Projects & Goals

Garden Tips

Harvest Green Tomatoes.

Harvest Sweet Potatoes.

Prepare Christmas Cactuses For Blooming.

Plant full grown Mums.

Plant Trees.

Plant Bulb Garden For Spring. Bring in potted Plants before a frost.

Cut back Oregano by half on each side.

Plant Garlic.

Personal Projects

- ☐ _____
- ☐ _____
- ☐ _____
- ☐ _____
- ☐ _____
- ☐ _____
- ☐ _____
- ☐ _____
- ☐ _____
- ☐ _____
- ☐ _____
- ☐ _____
- ☐ _____

Garden Projects

- ☐ _____
- ☐ _____
- ☐ _____
- ☐ _____
- ☐ _____
- ☐ _____
- ☐ _____
- ☐ _____
- ☐ _____
- ☐ _____
- ☐ _____
- ☐ _____
- ☐ _____

I'm Grateful For:

Month: _____

Weather
_____
_____
_____
_____
_____
_____

Sow	Plant	Harvest	Feed

Prune

The glory of gardening: hands in the dirt, head in the sun, heart with nature. To nurture a garden is to feed not just on the body, but the soul. Alfred Austin

JOB 1

Notes:

Notes:

JOB 2

_____

_____

_____

_____

_____

_____

_____

_____

_____

_____

_____

_____

_____

_____

Notes:

Notes:

JOB 3

Notes:

Notes:

JOB 4

Notes:

Notes:

JOB 5

Notes:

Notes:

Garden Notes

Notes:

Notes:

Garden Notes

Notes:

Notes:

NOVEMBER

AUTUMN LEAVES and Pumpkin PLEASE

Welcome to my Garden

November

Sun	Mon	Tues	Wed	Thurs	Fri	Sat

Important Notes & Reminders

_____

_____

_____

Goals For The Month Of November

Garden

- _____
- _____
- _____
- _____
- _____

Herbs

- _____
- _____
- _____
- _____
- _____

Family

- _____
- _____
- _____
- _____
- _____

Home

- _____
- _____
- _____
- _____
- _____

Clean It Up

- _____
- _____
- _____
- _____
- _____

Rewards

- _____
- _____
- _____
- _____
- _____

Health

- _____
- _____
- _____
- _____
- _____

Best Things That Happened!

_____

_____

_____

_____

_____

November Garden Tips, Projects & Goals

Garden Tips

Clean up garden, Fall Plow.

Remove Leaves from lawn.

Build a Compost Heap.

Move Houseplants closer to sunny window. Water less.

Collect seeds from flowers and store.

Cut Mums Back to Ground level.

Cut roses back.
Mulch Strawberry plants.

Personal Projects

- [ ] _____
- [ ] _____
- [ ] _____
- [ ] _____
- [ ] _____
- [ ] _____
- [ ] _____
- [ ] _____
- [ ] _____
- [ ] _____
- [ ] _____
- [ ] _____
- [ ] _____

Garden Projects

- [ ] _____
- [ ] _____
- [ ] _____
- [ ] _____
- [ ] _____
- [ ] _____
- [ ] _____
- [ ] _____
- [ ] _____
- [ ] _____
- [ ] _____
- [ ] _____
- [ ] _____

I'm Grateful For:

 Month: _____

Weather
_____
_____
_____
_____
_____
_____

Sow	Plant	Harvest	Feed
			Prune

Autumn is a second spring when every leaf is a flower.
Albert Camus

 JOB 1

Notes:

Notes:

JOB 2

Notes:

Notes:

JOB 3

_____

_____

_____

_____

_____

_____

_____

_____

_____

_____

_____

_____

_____

_____

_____

_____

Notes:

Notes:

JOB 4

Notes:

Notes:

JOB 5

_____

_____

_____

_____

_____

_____

_____

_____

_____

_____

_____

_____

_____

_____

_____

Notes:

Notes:

Garden Notes

Notes:

Notes:

Garden Notes

Notes:

Notes:

Garden Notes

Notes:

Notes:

WINTER

Welcome to my Garden

Winter Tasks

Date	To Do	Done
		☐
		☐
		☐
		☐
		☐
		☐
		☐
		☐
		☐
		☐
		☐
		☐
		☐
		☐

Notes:

Winter Tasks

Date	To Do	Done
_____	_____	☐
_____	_____	☐
_____	_____	☐
_____	_____	☐
_____	_____	☐
_____	_____	☐
_____	_____	☐
_____	_____	☐
_____	_____	☐
_____	_____	☐
_____	_____	☐
_____	_____	☐
_____	_____	☐
_____	_____	☐

Notes:

Garden Notes

Notes:

Notes:

DECEMBER

Welcome to my Garden

December

Sun	Mon	Tues	Wed	Thurs	Fri	Sat

Important Notes & Reminders

_____

_____

_____

_____

Goals For The Month Of December

Garden
- _____
- _____
- _____
- _____
- _____

Herbs
- _____
- _____
- _____
- _____
- _____

Family
- _____
- _____
- _____
- _____
- _____

Home
- _____
- _____
- _____
- _____
- _____

Clean It Up
- _____
- _____
- _____
- _____
- _____

Rewards
- _____
- _____
- _____
- _____
- _____

Health
- _____
- _____
- _____
- _____
- _____

Best Things That Happened!
_____
_____
_____
_____

December Garden Tips, Projects & Goals

Garden Tips
Prune Hollies.
Mulch over Mums and Foxglove.
Prepare sunny location for Christmas Plants.
Toss ashes from fireplace onto the garden.
Continue feeding the birds outside.
Check houseplants for spider mites.
Bring in Rosemary plant.
Slip some Rosemary Sprigs in with Christmas Cards.
"rosemary for remembrance"

Personal Projects

❑ _____
❑ _____
❑ _____
❑ _____
❑ _____
❑ _____
❑ _____
❑ _____
❑ _____
❑ _____
❑ _____
❑ _____
❑ _____

Garden Projects

❑ _____
❑ _____
❑ _____
❑ _____
❑ _____
❑ _____
❑ _____
❑ _____
❑ _____
❑ _____
❑ _____
❑ _____
❑ _____

I'm Grateful For:

Month: _____

Weather
_____
_____
_____
_____
_____
_____

Sow	Plant	Harvest	Feed

Prune

A garden must combine the poetic and the mysterious with a feeling of serenity and joy.
Luis Barragan

JOB 1

_____

_____

_____

_____

_____

_____

_____

_____

_____

_____

_____

_____

_____

Notes: Notes:

JOB 2

_____

_____

_____

_____

_____

_____

_____

_____

_____

_____

_____

_____

_____

_____

Notes:

Notes:

JOB 3

Notes:

Notes:

JOB 4

Notes:

Notes:

JOB 5

Notes:

Notes:

Garden Notes

Notes:

Notes:

PLANT CARE

Welcome to my Garden

Problem Log

Date	Plant	Problem	Treatment

Pests and Diseases Tracker

Date	I.D.	Problem	Treatment	Notes

Pest Control

BED/ROW	CROP/FAMILY	PEST	DISEASE	TREATMENT:

Garden Care Notes

Garden Care Notes

HARVESTING

Welcome to my Garden

Harvest Record

Year: _____

Date	Harvested	Yield	Done
_____	_____	_____	☐
_____	_____	_____	☐
_____	_____	_____	☐
_____	_____	_____	☐
_____	_____	_____	☐
_____	_____	_____	☐
_____	_____	_____	☐
_____	_____	_____	☐
_____	_____	_____	☐
_____	_____	_____	☐
_____	_____	_____	☐
_____	_____	_____	☐
_____	_____	_____	☐
_____	_____	_____	☐

Notes:

Notes:

Harvest Record

Year: _____

Date	Harvested	Yield	Done
_____	_____	_____	☐
_____	_____	_____	☐
_____	_____	_____	☐
_____	_____	_____	☐
_____	_____	_____	☐
_____	_____	_____	☐
_____	_____	_____	☐
_____	_____	_____	☐
_____	_____	_____	☐
_____	_____	_____	☐
_____	_____	_____	☐
_____	_____	_____	☐
_____	_____	_____	☐
_____	_____	_____	☐

Notes:

Notes:

Harvest Record

Year: _____

Date	Harvested	Yield	Done
_____	_____	_____	☐
_____	_____	_____	☐
_____	_____	_____	☐
_____	_____	_____	☐
_____	_____	_____	☐
_____	_____	_____	☐
_____	_____	_____	☐
_____	_____	_____	☐
_____	_____	_____	☐
_____	_____	_____	☐
_____	_____	_____	☐
_____	_____	_____	☐
_____	_____	_____	☐
_____	_____	_____	☐

Notes:

Notes:

Seed Saving Log

Seed	Company	Yield	Saved
			☐
			☐
			☐
			☐
			☐
			☐
			☐
			☐
			☐
			☐
			☐
			☐
			☐
			☐
			☐

Plants Planted This Year

Year _____

Date	Plant	Location	Notes

My Journal

Welcome to my Garden

Journal

DATE_____

Journal

DATE

Journal

DATE_____

Journal

DATE_____

 Journal

DATE_____

Journal

DATE_____

Journal

DATE_____

Journal

DATE _____

Journal

DATE_____

 Journal

DATE

Journal

DATE_____

Journal

DATE_____

Journal

DATE_____

WEATHER RECORDS

Welcome to my Garden

Weather Notes For Next Year

DATE_____

Annual Rainfall Chart

	J	F	M	A	M	J	J	A	S	O	N	D
1												
2												
3												
4												
5												
6												
7												
8												
9												
10												
11												
12												
13												
14												
15												
16												
Subtotal												

Annual Rainfall Chart

	J	F	M	A	M	J	J	A	S	O	N	D
17												
18												
19												
20												
21												
22												
23												
24												
25												
26												
27												
28												
29												
30												
31												
Total												

Weather Log

	J	F	M	A	M	J	J	A	S	O	N	D
1												
2												
3												
4												
5												
6												
7												
8												
9												
10												
11												
12												
13												
14												
15												
16												
Subtotal												

Weather Log

	J	F	M	A	M	J	J	A	S	O	N	D
17												
18												
19												
20												
21												
22												
23												
24												
25												
26												
27												
28												
29												
30												
31												
Total												

YEAR END NOTES

Welcome to my Garden

Highlights *Winners & Losers*

DATE_____

_____
_____
_____
_____
_____
_____
_____
_____
_____
_____
_____
_____
_____
_____
_____
_____
_____
_____
_____
_____
_____
_____
_____
_____
_____
_____

Things To Remember For Next Year

DATE_____

Things To Remember For Next Year

DATE_____

Ideas For Next Year's Garden

DATE_____

Ideas For Next Year's Garden

DATE_____

MY
GARDEN
♥
PLANNER
JOURNAL AND LOG BOOK

By
ENDLESS JOURNALS
https://endlessjournals.com

Made in United States
Orlando, FL
08 January 2022

13147822R00150